Generis
PUBLISHING

Gender Inequality in Georgia's Labour Market

Mariam Okruashvili
Khatia Tsaava

Title: **Gender Inequality in Georgia's Labour Market**

ISBN: 979-8-89248-739-9

Author: Mariam Okruashvili, Khatia Tsaava

Cover image: www.pixabay.com

Publisher: Generis Publishing
Online orders: www.generis-publishing.com
Contact email: info@generis-publishing.com

Gender Inequality in Georgia's Labour Market

This book examines gender inequality in Georgia's labour market, focusing on wage disparities, employment gaps, and unpaid work. Using data analysis and statistical modelling, it highlights the economic and social impacts of gender-based inequities, addressing both cultural and policy-driven factors. By exploring these dynamics, the study offers insights into the barriers women face in achieving economic equality and underscores the need for targeted reforms to foster a more inclusive labour market.

Mariam Okruashvili, Khatia Tsaava

Contents

List of Tables, Graphs, and Maps

Tables

Graphs

Maps

List of Abbreviations

SDG	Sustainable Development Goal
Un Women	United Nations Entity for Gender Equality and the Empowerment of Women
Geostat	National Statistics Office of Georgia
ICT	Information and Communication Technologies
LFS	Labour Force Survey
TUS	Time Use Survey
GEL	Georgian Lari

Introduction

This study aims to analyse statisticaly gender inequality in Georgia, primarily focusing on the labour market, where gender disparities are especially pressing. Achieving gender equality is a fundamental human right and essential for fostering a peaceful, inclusive, and sustainable society. Gender equality is the 5th Sustainable Development Goal (SDG), underscoring its global importance. While many countries, including Georgia, have made progress in addressing gender disparities, the social and economic effects of the COVID-19 pandemic have intensified these inequalities, reversing some advancements from previous decades. Addressing these challenges requires sustained efforts, including promoting gender-sensitive laws, policies, and institutional reforms (UN Women, n.d.).

Gender-related data must be improved and developed to track advancement and determine the extent of disparity. Wide-ranging data allows the identification of trends and provides insights for policymakers and advocates to develop effective strategies. This, in turn, helps to formulate policies that can eventually reduce gender inequality, especially in the labour market. By improving the social and economic status of women and girls, efforts to address gender disparities also contribute to the broader goals of poverty reduction and improving general well-being within society.

In Georgia, gender imbalance is most evident in the labour market, where significant differences exist in wages, unemployment, and the division of paid and unpaid work. These disparities are a serious social and economic issue, as they limit the country's overall potential for growth and development. Unemployment, a key indicator of economic instability, mainly affects women and contributes to broader issues of poverty and social inequality. Moreover, the gender ratio among the economically inactive population and the uneven distribution of unpaid work within households intensify women's challenges face in achieving economic independence.

Historically, Georgian society has been shaped by patriarchal norms that assign distinct roles to men and women, with women traditionally confined to domestic duties and men occupying positions of economic and social power. Although significant legal progress has been made in recent years, with the adoption of the Law on Gender Equality (2010) and the National Action Plan for Gender Equality, these changes have not yet fully translated into equality in the labour market.

Today, the gender wage gap remains a persistent issue in Georgia. Women are primarily employed in lower-paying sectors such as education, healthcare, and service industries, while men dominate higher-paying fields like technology, finance, and engineering. Additionally, women bear the brunt of unpaid care work, such as household management and caregiving for children and older people. These imbalances limit women's opportunities for professional advancement and perpetuate economic inequality. The COVID-19 pandemic further highlighted these issues, as women disproportionately lost jobs and took on more unpaid caregiving duties during lockdowns.

International comparisons reveal that Georgia faces challenges similar to many other post-Soviet countries, where progress toward gender equality has been uneven. While Georgia performs better than some of its regional neighbors regarding women's educational attainment and participation in the workforce, it lags behind global leaders. Countries that consistently rank highest in gender equality, such as those in Scandinavia, have achieved significant progress through comprehensive social policies, including paid parental leave, universal childcare, and strong labour protections—largely absent policies in Georgia.

Cultural factors also play a significant role in perpetuating gender inequality. Traditional gender norms remain deeply ingrained, particularly in rural areas, where women are often expected to prioritize family responsibilities over their careers. This social pressure limits their participation in the labour market and stunts their career growth. Moreover, issues such as domestic violence and gender-based discrimination, though increasingly addressed in public discourse, remain prevalent, with many cases going unreported or inadequately handled by authorities.

Despite these challenges, there are positive signs of change. Recent reforms to improve gender equality and the growing involvement of civil society organizations and international organisations like UN Women have fostered increased awareness of the issue. Gender-sensitive budgeting and policy initiatives have begun to gain traction, aiming to ensure that public funds are used in ways that promote equality. Moreover, public awareness campaigns are challenging traditional gender roles, particularly among younger generations, which may lead to a shift in social attitudes over time.

To sum up, while gender inequality in Georgia has deep historical and cultural roots, there is potential for progress. Addressing the disparities in the labour market will require legal reforms and a shift in social attitudes toward gender roles. Improving gender-related statistics and data collection will be essential in understanding the full scope of the issue and developing effective solutions. By focusing on policy reforms and changing social norms, Georgia can make strides toward reducing gender inequality and achieving a more equitable society.

Gender Inequality in the Labour Market of Georgia: Factors, Wage Gaps, and Sectoral Disparities

Gender inequality in the labour market is a global issue, and Georgia is no exception. This disparity significantly prevents the country's economic growth and negatively impacts individual and collective well-being. Despite existing legislation aimed at preventing gender discrimination, inequalities persist—both directly and indirectly—in the labour market.

One of the primary drivers of gender inequality is the disproportionate burden of unpaid work, which overwhelmingly falls on women. Studies on time use conducted across various countries reveal that, on average, women spend two to three times more hours per day on unpaid work than men. In Georgia, this gap is even more conspicuous, with women spending 4.8 times more hours on unpaid care and domestic work than men. This high involvement in unpaid activities is a crucial factor in the underrepresentation of women in the labour force and their higher economic inactivity rates. Even when women participate in the labour market, they are often employed with fewer working hours. According to 2023 data, the average number of hours men work per week in their main job is 13.6 percent higher than that of women (Geostat, Employment and Unemployment, 2023). This difference in working hours is one of the primary contributors to wage inequality.

Average Monthly Nominal Wages

In addition to the disparities in working hours, the wage gap is heavily influenced by job roles and hierarchical positions. Men are disproportionately represented in higher-paying and senior-level positions, further aggravating wage inequality between genders. One of the most significant manifestations of gender inequality in Georgia's labour market is the wage gap. Despite laws prohibiting all forms of discrimination—including gender-based discrimination—and the active involvement of international organizations, the wage disparity remains extensive.

Georgia is a member of the Equal Pay International Coalition, which advocates for equal wages for equal work. However, in 2022, the average monthly nominal wage for men in formal jobs was 46.4 percent higher than that of women. This gender wage gap is particularly unambiguous in specific sectors. For instance, in financial and insurance activities, the wage gap reaches 77.8 percent, even though salaries in this sector are relatively high for both men and women.

The graph below shows the average monthly nominal wages of hired employees by gender.

Graph 1: Average Monthly Nominal Wages of Hired Employees by Gender (GEL)

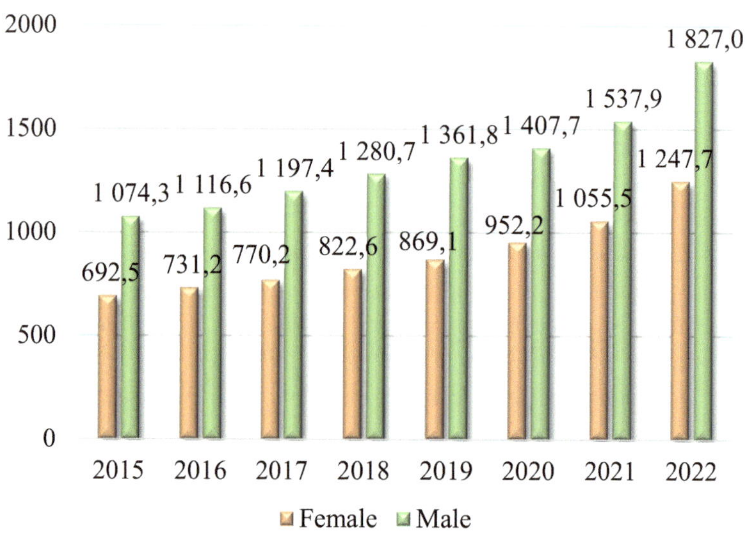

Source: Geostat

As evidenced by the data, the average monthly nominal wages from 2015 to 2022 show a consistent upward trend for both women and men. Over this period, the average absolute increase was 79.3 GEL for women and 107.5 GEL for men. The most significant wage increase occurred in 2022, when women saw an average rise of 192.2 GEL, while men experienced a higher increase of 289.1 GEL. Although the absolute increase was notably different by gender, the percentage growth rates were nearly equal, with women's wages increasing by 18.2 percent and men's wages - by 18.8 percent. This suggests that, despite the gender wage gap, the proportional wage growth remained equal across genders.

ICT Skills and Wage Impact

Possessing various skills in Information and Communication Technologies (ICT) is crucial in determining the average monthly nominal wages of hired employees. These skills align with SDG indicator 4.4.1, calculated based on survey on a ICT usage in households.

This indicator has been calculated by gender using anonymized data from the 2019–2023 survey on ICT usage in households. The table below illustrates the proportion of youth and adults (aged 15 and older) who possess ICT skills, categorized by skill type and gender. The data highlights the significance of ICT proficiency in shaping employment opportunities and wage potential, especially in a rapidly digitizing economy.

Table 1: Proportion of Youth and Adults Aged 15 Years and Older with ICT Skills by Type of Skill and Gender (%)

	2022		2023	
	Women	**Men**	**Women**	**Men**
Copying or moving a file or folder	33.5	34.5	31.5	31.6
Using copy and paste tools to duplicate or move information within a document	33.5	34.2	31.5	32.1
Sending e-mails with attached files (e.g., document, picture, video)	35.0	35.6	37.2	38.2
Using basic arithmetic formulas in a spreadsheet	9.4	9.6	8.5	9.4
Connecting and installing new devices (e.g., a modem, camera, printer)	13.1	19.7	13.2	17.2
Finding, downloading, installing, and configuring software	11.9	16.8	12.0	13.6
Creating electronic presentations with presentation software (including images, sound, video, or charts)	11.9	9.1	12.1	9.8
Transferring files between a computer and other devices	23.3	23.6	22.0	24.3

<u>Source:</u> *Calculated by the authors, based on an anonymized database from the survey on ICT usage in households.*

Notably, improvements in specific ICT skills significantly impact changes in the average monthly nominal wages. Correlation coefficients were calculated for 2019–2022 to assess the relationship between skill acquisition and wage growth. For women, the most significant factor affecting wage increases was the ability to use copy-and-paste tools to duplicate or move information within a document, with a correlation coefficient of 0.97. This indicates a solid positive relationship between this skill and wage growth. In contrast, for men, the highest correlation was found with the ability to find, download, install, and configure software products, yielding a correlation coefficient of 0.57, indicating a moderate positive relationship.

Wage Gap Dynamics Over Time

The graph below illustrates the differences in the average monthly nominal wages of women and men employees, further highlighting the persistent gender wage gap in Georgia's labour market.

Graph 2: Gender Wage Gap: Average Monthly Nominal Wages of Women and Men (GEL)

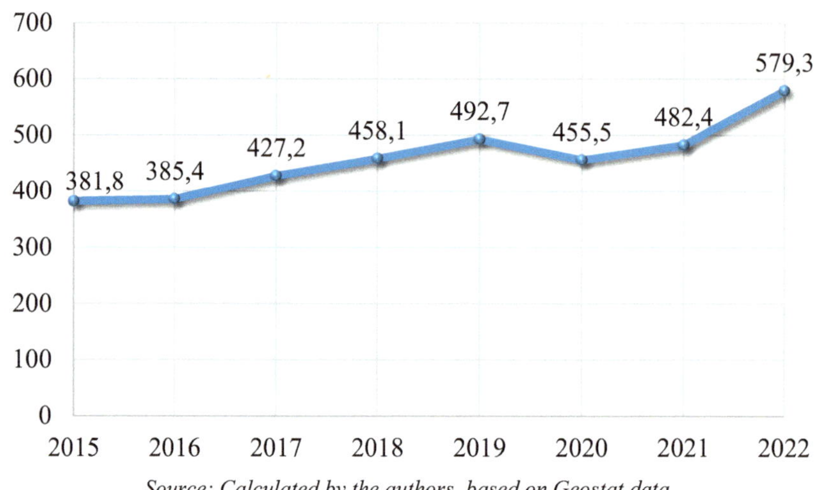

Source: Calculated by the authors, based on Geostat data.

Based on the data presented in the graph, the wage gap between women and men was at its narrowest in 2015, amounting to 381.8 GEL. The most significant gap was recorded in 2022, with a difference of 579.3 GEL. Despite this increase in absolute terms, the overall gender imbalance has decreased over time. In 2015, the average monthly wage of men was 55.1 percent higher than women's; by 2022, this difference had reduced to 46.4 percent.

Wages and Type of Economic Activity

The table below provides the average monthly nominal wages of hired employees by type of activity and gender.

Table 2: Average Monthly Nominal Wages of Hired Employees by Type of Economic Activity and Gender, 2022 (GEL)

	Women	Men
Agriculture, forestry, and fishing	854.5	1 149.1
Mining and quarrying	1 596.9	2 175.4
Manufacturing	1 078.6	1 728.2
Electricity, gas, steam, and air conditioning supply	1 918.2	1 787.0
Water supply, sewerage, waste management, and remediation activities	922.9	1 047.8
Construction	1 579.8	2 104.4
Wholesale and retail trade; repair of motor vehicles and motorcycles	1 050.8	1 674.9
Transportation and storage	1 423.5	1 754.2
Accommodation and food service activities	1 026.0	1 351.2
Information and communication	2 510.5	3 500.5
Financial and insurance activities	2 107.4	3 746.4
Real estate activities	1 375.0	1 546.4
Professional, scientific, and technical activities	1 855.9	2 759.4
Administrative and support service activities	1 033.9	1 141.2
Public administration and defence; compulsory social security	1 767.6	1 848.2
Education	936.4	960.2
Human health and social work activities	1 257.5	1 776.2
Arts, entertainment, and recreation	1 169.8	1 777.8
Other service activities	911.6	1 413.5
Total	**1 247.7**	**1 827.0**

Source: Geostat

Based on the data in the table, men's wages are higher than women's across all activities except for the electricity, gas, steam, and air conditioning sectors. The most pronounced gender imbalance occurs in financial and insurance activities, where both women and men receive relatively high wages. In this sector, the average monthly nominal wage for women is 2 107.4 GEL, while for men, it is 3 746.4 GEL, resulting in a wage inequality of 77.8 percent.

The next highest-paying sector for women and men is information and communications, with average monthly nominal wages of 2 510.5 GEL for women and 3 500.5 GEL for men. Conversely, one of the lowest-paying sectors is education, where most employees are women.

Regional Disparities in Wages

In addition to disparities across different types of activities, regional gender differences also warrant attention.

The table below presents the average monthly nominal wages of hired employees, categorised by region and gender.

Table 3: Average Monthly Nominal Wages by Region and Gender, 2022 (GEL)

Region	Total	Women	Men
Tbilisi	1 807.6	1 489.4	2 103.9
Adjara A.R.	1 194.8	988.9	1 401.5
Guria	880.9	776.6	1 001.3
Imereti	1 147.9	881.8	1 418.6
Kakheti	1 004.3	802.3	1 263.6
Mtskheta-Mtianeti	1 324.9	982.9	1 612.2
Racha-Lechkhumi and Kvemo Svaneti	823.7	712.6	947.9
Samegrelo-Zemo Svaneti	1 105.7	847.6	1 363.0
Samtskhe-Javakheti	1 008.0	832.9	1 195.5
Kvemo Kartli	1 263.8	929.6	1 540.6
Shida Kartli	990.1	796.9	1 217.0
Georgia	**1 543.0**	**1 247.7**	**1 827.0**

Based on the table above, the highest average wage for women and men is found in the capital city of Georgia, Tbilisi, the only region where salaries exceed the national average. Conversely, the lowest wages for both sexes are recorded in Racha-Lechkhumi and Kvemo Svaneti, with women earning an average of 712.6 GEL and men earning 947.9 GEL. In Guria, the average wages are slightly higher, at 776.6 GEL for women and 1 001.3 GEL for men.

In terms of gender inequality, the most significant disparity is observed in Kvemo Kartli, where the average monthly nominal wage of hired men surpasses that of women by 65.7 percent. Mtskheta-Mtianeti follows this at 64.0 percent and Imereti at 60.9 percent. Conversely, the lowest gender inequality is seen in Guria and Racha-Lechkhumi and Kvemo Svaneti, with disparities of 28.9 percent and 33.0 percent, respectively; however, it is essential to note that both regions also exhibit the lowest wages for both women and men.

Adjusted Gender Wage Gap

The gender inequality in wages can be attributed to various factors. One significant factor is the level of education achieved; however, in Georgia, it cannot be said that women lag behind men in educational attainment. Experience also plays a crucial role in influencing wage and employment status. According to the Labour Force Survey (LFS) database for 2023, the work experience rate for the unemployed over the past eight years was 10.2 percent for women and 11.4 percent for men. The adjusted gender wage gap considers these factors when analysing gender differences.

The gender wage gap provides a more accurate reflection of wage imbalances. The adjusted gender wage gap offers a more precise picture by accounting for a person's education, work experience, and other job-related characteristics. However, it is essential to acknowledge that it is nearly impossible to capture every relevant factor. For instance, the adjusted gender wage gap may not account for personal or labour market characteristics or unobservable traits such as motivation, dedication, attention, work ethic, and networking abilities.

The National Statistics Office of Georgia (Geostat) has calculated both hourly and monthly adjusted gender wage gaps. In 2022, the adjusted gender wage gap—hourly and monthly—was notably high, varying by type of activity and the positions held. The monthly wage disparity typically exceeds the hourly difference, mainly due to the fewer hours women work.

The chart below presents the adjusted gender wage gap for 2022, categorised by job position.

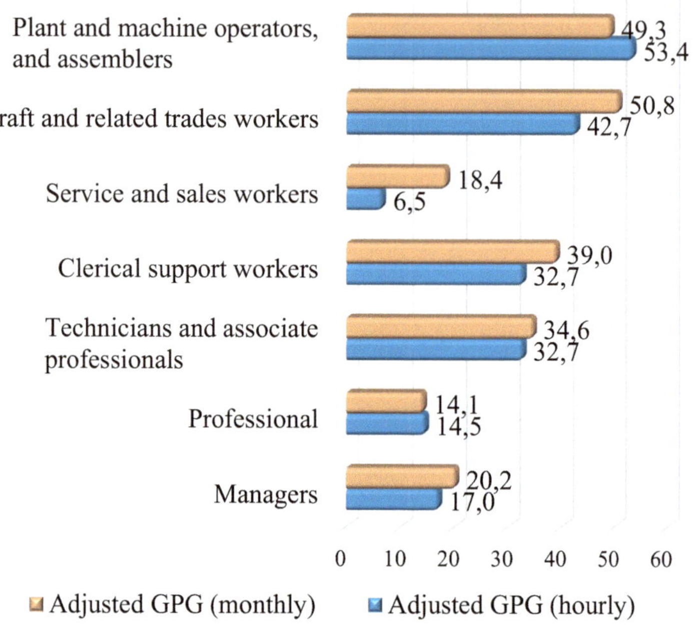

Source: Geostat

Gender Inequality in the Labour Market: Employment and GDP, Socio-economic Factors

For a more in-depth analysis of gender imbalance in the labour market, it is essential to consider the system of indicators calculated within the framework of the LFS. In 2023, the number of women aged 15 and older is projected to be 16.6 percent higher than that of men in the same age group. However, the number of employed men exceeds that of women by 23.2 percent. This difference is primarily attributed to the population outside the labour force, with women comprising 65.6 percent. This is a significant factor contributing to the much lower unemployment rate among women compared to men (Geostat, Employment and Unemployment, 2023).

Employment Rate by Gender

The employment rate, defined as the ratio of employed individuals to the population aged 15 and older, is crucial to consider from a gender perspective.

The graph below illustrates the employment rate from 2015 to 2023, categorised by gender.

Graph 4: Employment Rate by Gender (%)

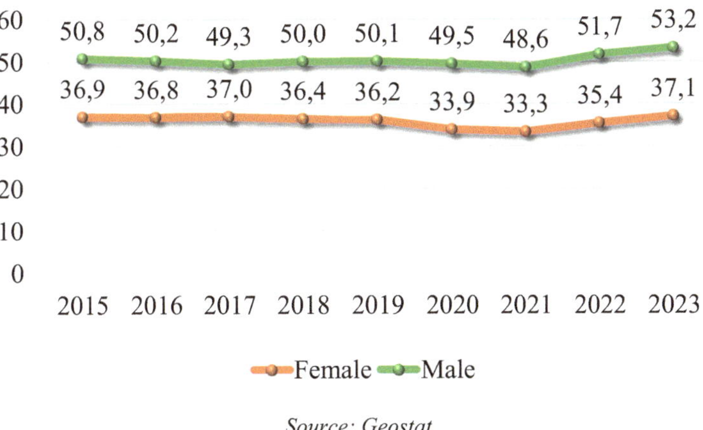

Source: Geostat

As illustrated in the graph, the employment level for men from 2015 to 2023 consistently exceeds that of women. The inequality becomes more pronounced between 2020 and 2023, with women and men experiencing their lowest employment rates in 2021. Compared to 2015, the number of employed women in 2021 has decreased by 3.6 percentage points, while the decline for men is 2.2 percentage points.

Unemployment Rate by Gender

Regarding the unemployment rate, the graph indicates that from 2015 to 2023, the unemployment rate for men is higher than that for women each year. This disparity is primarily attributed to the fact that the most unemployed women belong to the population outside the labour force. Consequently, they do not meet the criteria for unemployment, which includes being unemployed during the past seven days at the time of the survey, not having looked for a job during the past four weeks, or not being ready to start work within the next two weeks if offered a job.

The graph below displays the unemployment rate from 2015 to 2023, broken down by gender.

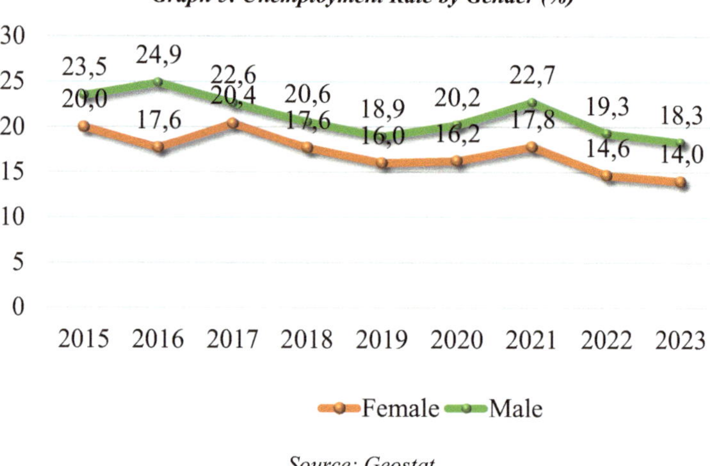

Graph 5: Unemployment Rate by Gender (%)

Source: Geostat

GDP and Unemployment

Gender inequality in the labour market significantly impacts the country's economic situation. To better understand this issue, it is crucial to examine the relationship between GDP and the number of individuals who are either unemployed or part of the economically inactive population.

Table 4: GDP and Unemployment by Gender

Year	GDP ($)	Unemployed, thousand		Gender ratio
		Women	Men	
2010	3 281.2	1 151.6	795.6	1.4
2011	4 120.8	1 145.6	759.5	1.5
2012	4 530.7	1 122.0	723.1	1.6
2013	4 711.8	1 094.6	744.5	1.5
2014	4 829.9	1 062.5	714.2	1.5
2015	4 085.1	1 022.6	688.0	1.5
2016	4 143.5	1 017.7	697.2	1.5
2017	4 420.3	1 014.6	710.8	1.4
2018	4 804.0	1 035.0	703.0	1.5
2019	4 741.4	1 036.3	704.9	1.5
2020	4 300.8	1 067.1	709.6	1.5
2021	5 083.6	1 072.9	720.0	1.5
2022	6 731.2	1 036.7	668.5	1.6
2023	8 218.8	1 015.4	647.1	1.6

Notably, for both genders, GDP shows a generally increasing trend, while the number of unemployed individuals tends to decrease. Additionally, the relationship between GDP and the number of unemployed men is more vital than that of women. The correlation coefficient for men is -0.8, indicating a strong negative relationship, whereas for women, it is -0.5, reflecting a more moderate connection.

Given the above, the high unemployment rate, especially when viewed through a gendered lens, significantly negatively impacts on the country's economic situation and the overall well-being of its population. Various socio-economic factors influence this. A key issue is the high rate of economically inactive individuals, particularly women, which is mainly due to their significant involvement in unpaid domestic and care work. Attention must be drawn to the fact that many mothers need help to engage in paid work due to their caregiving responsibilities.

Socio-economic Factors: Maternity Leave and Childcare Issues

A critical aspect of this situation is the duration of leave for pregnancy, childbirth, child care, and adoption, which is set at 730 days, with only 183 days being paid (or 200 days in cases of twins or complications). In a country where most families fall within the low-income to middle-income brackets, it is often difficult for any family member to take unpaid maternity leave, as their income is essential for meeting basic needs. This forces many families to make difficult choices. In most cases, mothers are compelled to take unpaid maternity leave, or families hire nannies whose salaries may exceed the mother's income. Women often make these compromises in the private sector because they fear losing their jobs.

Additionally, it is common for other family members, such as grandmothers, to assume child-rearing responsibilities. This often results in older women who previously held low-paying jobs leaving the workforce to care for grandchildren. While this arrangement can work for some families, it raises concerns about whether it is appropriate for any family member to forgo their income to perform unpaid and highly demanding care work.

This issue is particularly pressing in Georgia, making it crucial for the state to develop mechanisms that support working parents, especially those with newborns. One potential solution is the establishment of affordable childcare facilities for children six months and older, enabling parents to return to work. Such services should be low-cost and accessible to all. Additionally, there is a need to adjust the working hours of public kindergartens to better align with parents' work schedules. Public institutions offer parents only a half-hour concession in the morning or evening, which is insufficient, especially for those working in the private sector, where such concessions are rarely available.

Addressing Gender Inequality: Remote Work Solutions

The COVID-19 pandemic has demonstrated that many services can effectively be delivered remotely. Therefore, offering flexible, remote work options for newborn parents could be another viable solution. Addressing this problem is vital not only for reducing gender inequality but also for improving the well-being of individual families. Moreover, it could positively impact the country's demographic situation.

The situation could be significantly improved if accessible and affordable childcare services for children under two years old were available. Furthermore, the flexibility of remote work, as proven during the pandemic, should be considered an option for mothers to balance work and caregiving.

According to LFS, it is important to assess the number of employees who worked from home in the pre-pandemic, pandemic, and post-pandemic periods during the four weeks before the survey.

Table 5: Remote Working by Gender (%)

	2018		2020		2023	
	Women	Men	Women	Men	Women	Men
Yes, half the working days or more	3.1	1.7	8.3	3.0	5.0	2.4
Yes, less than half of the working days	3.0	1.3	2.6	1.6	1.7	1.0
No	94.0	96.9	89.1	95.4	93.3	96.6

<u>*Source:*</u> *Calculated by the authors, based on a database from the LFS.*

Of the employees surveyed in the pre-pandemic period, 6.1 percent of women and 3.0 percent of men worked from home in the preceding four weeks. Naturally, during the pandemic, this rate increased for both, rising to 10.9 percent for women and 4.6 percent for men. Even though remote work is feasible for many employees, the rate declined again in the post-pandemic period. By 2023, it had dropped to 6.7 percent for women and 3.4 percent for men. Nevertheless, this figure remains higher for both sexes than in the pre-pandemic period, indicating some progress.

Gender Inequality in the Labour Market: Disposable Wages, Gender-based Poverty and GDP

Beyond all the above mentioned issues, gender wage inequality remains a significant concern. Analyse considering disposable wages of women and men that are shown in the table below:

Table 6: Disposable Wage, by Gender, 2023 (%)

	Disposable Wage	
	Women	Men
100 GEL or less	39.2	60.8
101-150 GEL	61.1	38.9
151-200 GEL	69.4	30.6
201-300 GEL	63.6	36.4
301-400 GEL	71.3	28.7
401-500 GEL	66.0	34.0
501-600 GEL	65.7	34.3
601-800 GEL	56.7	43.3
801-1000 GEL	41.6	58.4
1001-1500 GEL	37.7	62.3
1501-2000 GEL	25.1	74.9
More than 2000 GEL	33.1	66.9

Source: Calculated by the authors, based on a database from the LFS.

The table shows that over half of the respondents (56.3%) reported a low disposable wage of 800 GEL or less. Notably, 63.2 percent of these respondents were women, while 36.8 percent were men. As wages increase, the proportion of men also rises, highlighting one of the main aspects of gender inequality in the labour market.

The disposable wage by gender (excluding income tax) is calculated from the 2023 LFS database. The average monthly disposable wage for women is 706.1 GEL, compared to 949.2 GEL for men. Additionally, it is essential to note the modal wage for both genders. The most significant number of women (69 307) reported their wages falling within the 601-800 GEL range, for which the modal value is 703.6 GEL. In contrast, most men (79 576) reported that their wage fluctuates between 1001-1500 GEL, with a modal value of 1100.1 GEL.

The situation is best reflected in the median disposable wages, which are 602.1 GEL for women and 871.4 GEL for men.

Graph 6: Average, Modal, and Median Disposable Wages by Gender, 2023 (GEL)

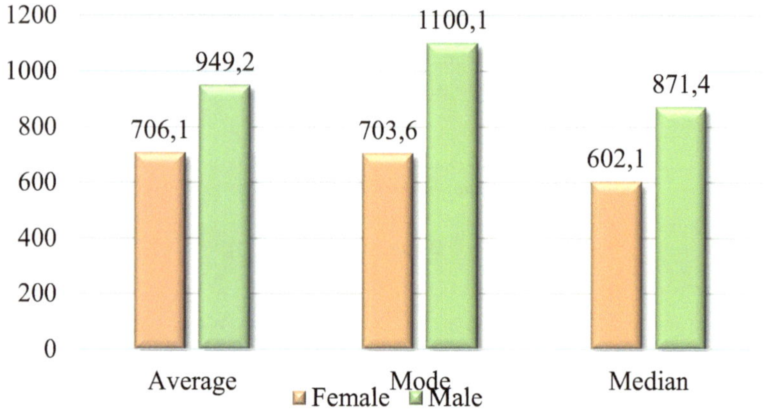

Source: Calculated by the authors, based on a database from the LFS.

The wages from primary employment in the last working month are the lowest in median wages for both genders, with a considerable gender gap across all three measures. Men's average wage surpasses women's by 34.4 percent, the modal wage by 56.4 percent, and the median wage by 44.7 percent.

Additionally, significant gender inequality persists in specific workplaces. For instance, women make comprise 71.5 percent of employees in household-based work settings, 61.1 percent in office jobs, and 61.0 percent in stores, kiosks, cafés, restaurants, and hotels. In contrast, men overwhelmingly dominate construction sites (99.6%), water bodies like reservoirs, lakes, rivers, and seas (99.3%), and transport (95.3%). This gender imbalance is partly driven by stereotypes, especially those related to suitable work environments for women and men, perceived differences in abilities, and other social factors.

Such disparities notably impact the national economy, underscoring the importance of examining the causal relationship between GDP and gender-based poverty.

Table 7: Share of population under absolute poverty by gender and GDP

Year	Under absolute poverty line (%)[1]		GDP[2]
	Women	Men	
2010	36.8	37.9	3 281.2
2011	34.0	34.3	4 120.8
2012	30.0	30.1	4 530.7
2013	25.8	26.7	4 711.8
2014	23.3	23.7	4 829.9
2015	21.3	22.0	4 085.1
2016	21.2	22.9	4 143.5
2017	21.6	22.4	4 420.3
2018	20.2	20.0	4 804.0
2019	19.4	19.6	4 741.4
2020	20.9	21.7	4 300.8
2021	17.1	17.9	5 083.6
2022	15.3	15.8	6 731.2
2023	11.5	12.2	8 218.8

[1]*Source: Absolute Poverty, Geostat*

[2]*Source: GDP, Geostat*

Based on the preceding table, poverty shows a decreasing trend for both genders, while GDP demonstrates an increasing trend. This indicates a negative correlation between these variables. Pearson's correlation coefficient is also harmful for both genders: -0.7 for men and women alike, suggesting a robust negative correlation between these variables. However, the correlation coefficient is 1.2 percent higher for men, implying that poverty levels impact GDP reduction more significantly for men and, conversely, poverty reduction influences GDP growth more strongly.

Econometric Analysis

The functioning of the labour market plays a critical role in shaping a country's economic situation. A linear regression model was constructed to explore this connection in more detail with GDP per capita as the dependent variable. The independent variables considered were the economic inactivity rate and wages. This model was analysed separately for women and men, revealing essential differences in how these factors influence economic performance.

Regression Model for Women

The econometric model for women indicates that GDP per capita has a negative relationship with the economic inactivity rate, while wages show a positive impact. The regression equation for women is:

$$\hat{y}_t = 6\,009.2 - 80.5x_{1t} + 3.9x_{2t}$$

Where:

- x_{1t} represents the economic inactivity rate;
- x_{2t} represents wages;
- $\hat{y}_t$ is the predicted GDP per capita.

In this equation, the coefficient $b_1 = -80.5$ reflects the average change in GDP resulting from a one-unit increase in the economic inactivity rate, assuming wages remain constant. This suggests that a higher inactivity rate reduces GDP. On the other hand, $b_2 = 3.9$ indicates that a one-unit increase in wages results in a modest increase in GDP, holding the inactivity rate constant.

While both variables influence GDP, the economic inactivity rate significantly impacts GDP per capita more than wages, as indicated by the magnitude of b_1 and b_2. However, comparing the coefficients directly is not straightforward due to their different units of measurement. To address this, we standardised the coefficients:

$$W_t = 6\,009.2 - 0.22z_{1t} + 0.95z_{2t}$$

This standardised form shows that wages have a significantly more substantial effect on GDP than the inactivity rate, with a more pronounced positive relationship between wages and economic performance.

Statistical Significance and Model Evaluation

To assess the statistical significance of the coefficients, we performed a t-test. The calculated t-value for the wage coefficient (t_{b_2}) was more significant than the critical value, indicating that this coefficient is statistically significant at the 5 percent significance level. In contrast, the inactivity rate coefficient was insignificant, as its t-value did not exceed the critical value. Nonetheless, given the economic relevance of the inactivity rate, it remains a critical factor in the model.

The 95 percent confidence intervals for these coefficients are:

$$-10\ 162.97 < B_0 < 22\ 181.35$$
$$-405.64 < B_1 < 244.66$$
$$0.19 < B_2 < 7.56$$

The third confidence interval for the wage coefficient excludes zero, further supporting the conclusion that wages significantly impact GDP.

The overall significance of the model was tested using the F-test, which produced an F-value of 5.22, exceeding the critical value of 5.14. This confirms that the regression equation as a whole is significant. The model's coefficient of determination (R^2) was 0.8, indicating that the economic inactivity rate and wages explain a substantial portion of the variation in GDP per capita. However, to account for the number of explanatory variables, the adjusted R^2 was 0.5, still indicating a good fit.

Regression Model for Men

A similar analysis was conducted for men, yielding the following regression equation:

$$\hat{y}_t = 5\ 524.6 - 126.3x_{1t} + 2.9x_{2t}$$

In this case, the economic inactivity rate has a more substantial negative effect on GDP than wages, with $b_1 = -126.3$ and $b_2 = 2.9$. These coefficients suggest that a higher inactivity rate leads to a more significant reduction in GDP for men, while an increase in wages has a more minor positive effect.

As with the model for women, we standardised the coefficients for comparability:

$$W_t = 5\ 524.6 - 0.29z_{1t} + 0.95z_{2t}$$

Again, this shows that wages substantially impact GDP more than the inactivity rate.

Statistical Significance and Model Evaluation

The t-test results indicated that only the wage coefficient (t_{b_2}) was statistically significant, with a t-value greater than the critical value. The confidence intervals for the coefficients were:

The 95 percent confidence intervals for these coefficients are:

$$-3\,763.8 < B_0 < 14\,812.98$$
$$-415.12 < B_1 < 162.62$$
$$0.92 < B_2 < 4.92$$

Again, the interval for the wage coefficient excludes zero, confirming its statistical significance.

The overall model for men was also evaluated using the F-test, which produced an F-value of 6.8, surpassing the critical value of 5.14. The coefficient of determination for the model was 0.83, indicating a solid fit, while the adjusted R^2 was 0.6, which also suggests that the model is robust despite including multiple explanatory variables.

Both the models for women and men illustrate the significant impact of economic inactivity and wages on GDP per capita. For both genders, wages exhibit a positive relationship with GDP, while economic inactivity has a negative effect. However, the magnitude of these effects differs between genders, with the economic inactivity rate playing a more substantial role for men and wages being more influential for women.

These findings highlight the importance of addressing gender-based disparities in the labour market, particularly in terms of economic inactivity and wage inequality, as these factors significantly affect national economic performance.

Unpaid Work in the Labour Market: A Gender-based Perspective in Georgia

To deepen the understanding of gender inequality in the labour market, it is essential to explore the critical issue of unpaid work, which remains a significant concern in Georgia. The share of time dedicated to unpaid care and domestic work is crucial for measuring gender equality, specifically under the SDG indicator 5.4.1. This indicator highlights the proportion of time spent on unpaid domestic and care work by sex, age, and location. To assess this, a comprehensive Time Use Survey (TUS) was conducted by Geostat with the financial and technical support of UN Women.

The survey, which covered 3,680 households across the country, involved 6 074 respondents who completed two time-use diaries—one for a weekday and another for a weekend day. The sample yielded 5 721 diaries for weekdays and 5 713 for weekends. The goal was to capture the amount of time people devote to various activities, including paid and unpaid work, caregiving, domestic duties, travel, and other daily activities. Additionally, the survey contributed valuable data to refine other SDG indicators, supporting the development of gender statistics (Un Women & Geostat, 2020-2021).

Conducted in 2020–2021, during the COVID-19 pandemic, the survey was influenced by the unique circumstances of that period. With strict movement restrictions, the timing of activities and participation in various tasks varied significantly. Education shifted to remote formats, most workplaces transitioned to remote working mode, and social interactions were drastically reduced. These factors profoundly impacted on how time was allocated, both in terms of paid work and unpaid domestic and care responsibilities. These changes must be considered when interpreting the survey results.

Enhancing Gender Statistics in Georgia

The findings of this survey have significantly enhanced gender statistics produced in the country, as demonstrated by the Open Data Watch results. According to Open Data Watch, gender statistics in the country are evaluated based on five main criteria: *availability*, which assesses the accessibility of 53 indicators on both the

National Statistics Office and other government websites; _openness_, which defines access and usage barriers to gender data; _institutional foundations_, which are legal, policy, and coordination frameworks supporting the collection, publication, and use of gender data; _capacity_, which reflects the country's technical and statistical ability to manage and maintain systems that produce gender data; and _funding_, which evaluates how well the national budget considers funds for gender statistics development, in addition to the significance of international support.

The TUS was pivotal role in improving Georgia's gender statistics framework. With the financial and technical backing of UN Women, the survey's results, released in 2022, contributed to the country's improved standing on the Open Data Watch gender statistics index. Georgia moved to fifth place out of 185 countries, reflecting significant progress in the development and transparency of gender data (Open Data Watch, 2023).

Time Allocation by Gender: Employment, Education, and Unpaid Work

In addition to measuring the SDG 5.4.1 indicator, "Proportion of time spent on unpaid domestic and care work, by sex, age, and location", it is equally important to assess how time is spent by gender on various activities, such as employment and related activities, production of goods for final consumption, unpaid household services provided for household and family members, unpaid caregiving services for household and family members, internships, voluntary and other forms of unpaid work, education, socialisation, and communication, participation in community and religious activities, cultural, recreational, sports, and media-related activities, personal care and self-maintenance, and more (Guerrero, 2020-2021).

The graph below presents time allocation by various activities among the Georgian population.

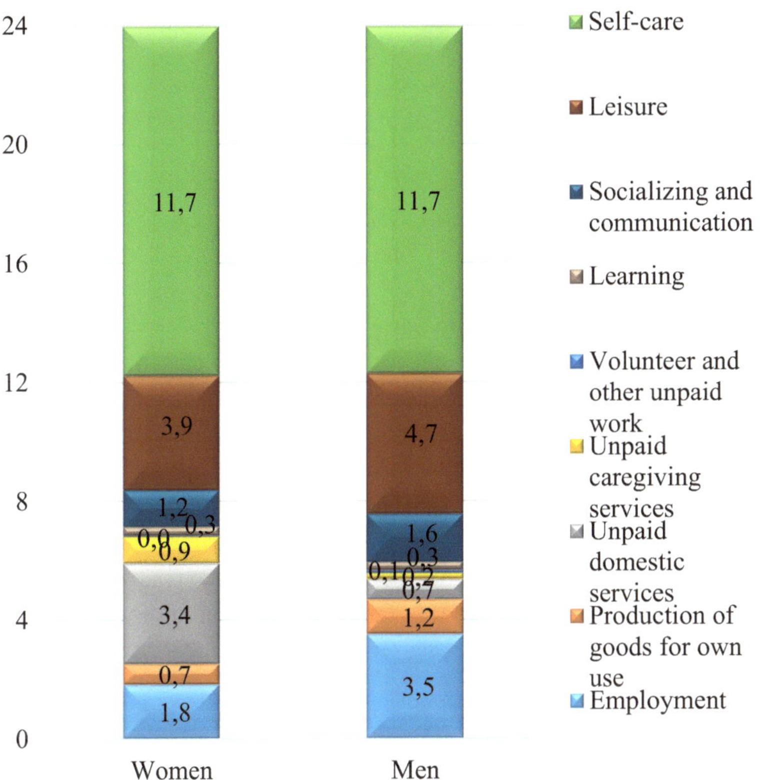

The indicators in the chart represent the average time the total population spends on various activities. In this context, particular focus should be placed on activities with a significant difference between the average time spent by the entire population and the average time spent by the population engaged in those activities. Therefore, among these activities, employment-related activities and education stand out as the most critical.

Women engaged in employment-related activities spend an average of 7.7 hours daily on these activities, while men spend an average of 8.6 hours daily. Regarding education, men and women spend an average of 0.3 hours daily. Women engaged in educational activities dedicate an average of 4.5 hours daily, and men spend 4.7 hours. The 15-24 age group is the most engaged in education and related activities, with 48.7 percent of women in this age group spending an average of 4.7 hours daily and 37.9

percent of men spending an average of 4.9 hours per day (Geostat, Time Use Survey in Georgia, 2020-2021).

Unpaid Domestic and Care Work: A Gender-based Divide

The SDG indicator 5.4.1 provides an essential lens to view gender disparities in the Georgian context. The indicator is determined by the time spent on unpaid domestic and care services for household and family members. Domestic services include tasks such as Food and meals management and preparation; cleaning and maintaining of own dwelling and surroundings; do-it-yourself decoration, maintenance, and repair; care and maintenance of textiles and footwear; household management for own final use; pet care; shopping for own household and family members; unpaid domestic services related travelling, moving, transporting or accompanying goods or persons related to unpaid domestic services for household and family members; and other unpaid domestic services for household and family members. Care services cover activities such as childcare and instruction; care for dependent adults; help to non-dependent adult household and family members; travelling and accompanying goods or persons related to unpaid caregiving services for household and family members; and other activities related to unpaid caregiving services for household and family members.

The graph below illustrates the proportion of time spent on unpaid care and domestic work by the Georgian population, broken down by type of settlement and gender.

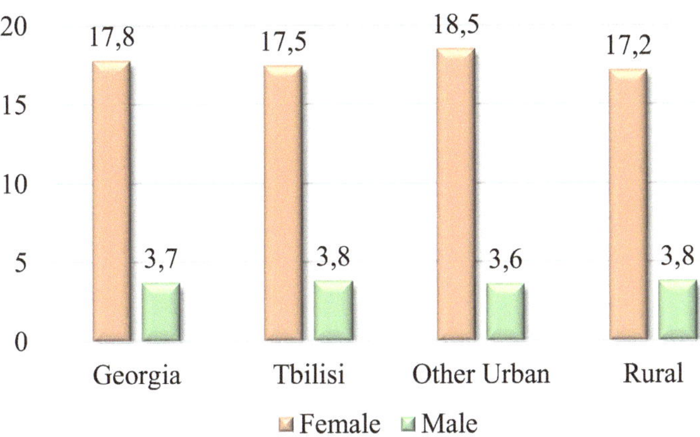

Source: Chart created by the authors, based on data from Geostat.

The survey findings reveal stark gender differences in time spent on unpaid domestic and care work. Women spend 17.8 percent of their day on unpaid labour, compared to just 3.7 percent for men. This translates into an average of 4.3 hours per day for women, which is 4.8 times greater than the 0.9 hours men spent. These disparities are particularly pronounced among women aged 25-44, who allocate an average of 5.5 hours per daily to unpaid work, while men in the same age group spend just 0.9 hours.

When broken down by region, women in Tbilisi spend 17.5 percent of their day on unpaid work, which is still significantly higher than the 3.8 percent men spent in the capital. This translates into an average of 4.2 hours daily for women, compared to 0.9 hours for men. Again, the 25-44 age group emerges as the most affected, with women spending an average of 5.3 hours per day on unpaid work, while men spend just 1.0 hours.

In other urban areas, women spend 18.5 percent of their day on unpaid labour, while men allocate 3.6 percent, corresponding to an average of 4.1 hours daily for women and 0.9 hours for men. The gendered gap persists, with women aged 25-44 in urban areas spending an average of 5.2 hours per day on unpaid work, compared to 1.0 hours for men.

The situation remains similar in rural areas, with women dedicating 17.2 percent of their day to unpaid work and men 3.8 percent. Women in rural areas spend an average of 4.4 hours daily on unpaid work, 5.1 times the 0.9 hours men spent. Women aged 25-44 in rural areas bear the highest burden, dedicating an average of 6.0 hours per day to unpaid labour, while men in the same group spend only 0.9 hours.

Econometric Analysis

To explore the factors influencing time spent on unpaid work in Georgia, a regression model was constructed with two independent variables: the highest education level attained and the current level of formal education. In this model, the dependent variable is the time dedicated to unpaid work. While employment status also significantly impacts unpaid work, its inclusion alongside education variables led to multicollinearity issues due to high correlation. Therefore, only educational attainment and current educational engagement were included as predictors.

Regression Model for Women

For women, the regression model is expressed as the following:

$$Y = 524.1 + 4.8X_1 - 45.7X_2$$

Where:

- X_1 represents the highest level of education attained;
- X_2 represents the current level of formal education;
- Y is the time spent on unpaid work.

According to this model, time spent on unpaid work is positively associated with the level of education attained (X_1) but negatively associated with the current level of formal education (X_2). While it might seem counterintuitive, higher educational attainment does not lessen women's household and caregiving responsibilities. Women with higher education levels may engage in these activities more earnestly, possibly due to social expectations or personal commitment. Conversely, those currently involved in formal education tend to spend less time on unpaid work, likely due to their studies' demands and time constraints.

The standardized coefficients, 0.04 for X_1 and -0.22 for X_2 indicate both variables' relatively small impact, though the negative effect of current education is more pronounced. Each coefficient is statistically significant at the 5 percent significance level, as shown by their respective t-values: $t_{crit} = 1.96$, $|t_{b_0}| = 28.3$, $|t_{b_1}| = 2.1$, and $|t_{b_2}| = 12.0$.

For coefficients B_0, B_1, and B_2, the 95 percent confidence intervals are as follows:

$$487.7 < B_0 < 560.4$$
$$0.3 < B_1 < 9.3$$
$$-53.2 < B_2 < -38.2$$

None of these intervals cover zero, supporting the rejection of the null hypothesis and indicating the meaningful impact of each predictor. The F-test confirms the model's overall validity, where the calculated F-value of 81.9 exceeds the critical threshold of 3.0, validating the model for drawing further conclusions about unpaid work among women in Georgia.

Regression Model for Men

For men, the regression model is structured as follows:

$$Y = 154.4 + 3.8X_1 - 10.2X_2,$$

where the variables retain the same definitions.

The model suggests a similar trend: time spent on unpaid work is positively associated with educational attainment (X_1) and negatively associated with current engagement in formal education (X_2). However, unlike the model for women, the influence of both education variables is notably weaker for men. Standardized coefficients of 0.07 for educational attainment and -0.09 for current education indicate a modest impact. Notably, women experience a more significant reduction in unpaid work time when engaged in formal education than men.

All three coefficients are statistically significant at the 5 percent significance level, as $|t_b| > t_{crit}$, where $t_{crit} = 1.96$, $|t_{b_0}| = 13.0$, $|t_{b_1}| = 2.5$, and $|t_{b_2}| = 3.5$.

For coefficients B_0, B_1, and B_2, the 95 percent confidence intervals are as follows:

$$131.1 < B_0 < 177.8$$
$$0.8 < B_1 < 6.8$$
$$-15.9 < B_2 < -4.4$$

As with the women's model, none of these intervals cover zero, reinforcing the significance of each variable in the model. The F-test for the men's regression model also confirms its validity, with an F-value of 11.2, surpassing the critical threshold of 3.0, thus allowing us to draw reliable conclusions from the model.

The SDG 5.4.1 Indicator and Regional Disparities in Unpaid Work in Georgia

Using data from the TUS, the SDG 5.4.1 indicator was calculated to measure the share of time spent on unpaid care and household work across settlement types, gender, and age groups. This analysis provides valuable insights into regional disparities in unpaid work within Georgia. Using anonymised data, we calculated the SDG 5.4.1 indicator by region and gender, applying the following formula.

$$\frac{5}{7} \times \frac{\text{Total time spent on activity 'X' across all weekday diary days}}{\text{Total count of all weekday diaries}} +$$

$$+ \frac{2}{7} \times \frac{\text{Total time spent on activity 'X' across all weekend diary days}}{\text{Total count of all weekend diaries}}$$

The percentage of time spent on these activities, relative to 24 hours, shows how much of the day the entire population (regardless of whether they are involved in these activities or not) spends on unpaid work.

These indicators are displayed on the Georgia map by region and gender to present a clearer analysis of the share of time spent on unpaid care and household work.

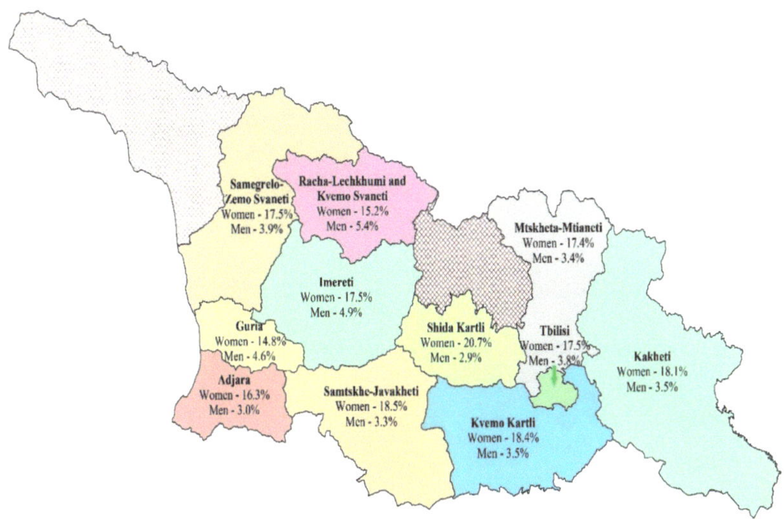

Note: Information is not available for the population living in the occupied territories of Georgia (the Autonomous Republic of Abkhazia and the Tskhinvali region).

Source: Calculated by the authors based on the anonymised database of the Time Use Survey.

This map reveals distinct patterns in unpaid work time across regions. Women in Shida Kartli dedicate the most time to unpaid work, averaging 5.0 hours daily, or 20.7 percent of a 24-hour day. In Samtskhe-Javakheti and Kvemo Kartli, women spend around 4.4 hours daily on unpaid work, which accounts for 18.5 percent and 18.4 percent of their day, respectively. In these same regions, men's unpaid work time is significantly lower—0.7 hours per day in Shida Kartli and 0.8 hours in Kvemo Kartli and Samtskhe-Javakheti. This imbalance translates to substantial gender inequality in unpaid work. Women in Shida Kartli perform unpaid work at 7.2 times the rate of men, while in Kvemo Kartli and Samtskhe-Javakheti, the disparity is 5.3 and 5.6 times, respectively. This inequality is partly attributed to high agricultural engagement in Shida Kartli, where men contribute 56.9 percent more time to household production than women, reflecting a daily difference of approximately 0.23 hours.

The pronounced gender disparity in unpaid work across these regions underscores an inefficient use of human capital, which negatively impacts the economy and individual well-being. Using data from the TUS and LFS, we estimated economic losses attributable to unpaid work among the economically inactive and unemployed.

Economic Impact of Gender Disparities in Unpaid Work and Inactivity

The TUS (conducted between 2020 and 2021) and median labour wages data from the 2021 LFS reveal significant income losses due to unpaid work. Median monthly disposable wages for women and men in 2021 were 450.9 GEL and 632.5 GEL, respectively. The economically inactive female population in 2021 was 956 902, compared to 519 750 for men. Considering median wages, women lose approximately 431.4 million GEL monthly, and men 328.7 million GEL. Although men's median wages surpass women's by 40.3 percent, total lost wages for women are 31.2 percent higher.

The graph below displays the median disposable labour wages for 2021.

Graph 9: Median Disposable Labour Wages, 2021 (GEL)

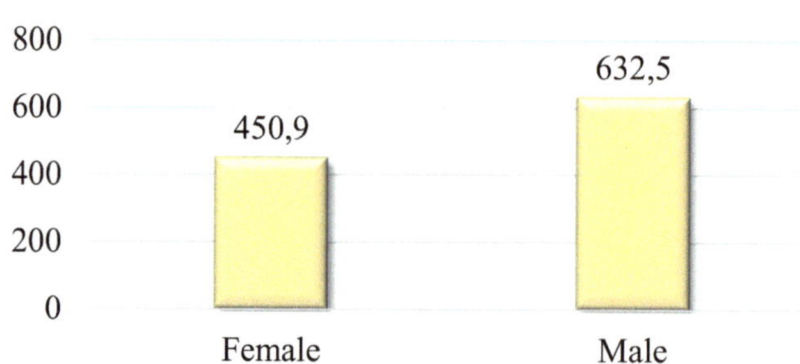

Source: Calculated by the authors based on a database of the LFS.

For unemployed individuals, estimated monthly losses are 483.7 million GEL for women and 455.4 million GEL for men. Additionally, full-time employed women face substantial income losses from unpaid work. On average, women spend 2.7 hours per day on unpaid work compared to men's 0.5 hours (Guerrero, 2020-2021), totalling 18.9 hours per week for women and 3.5 hours for men. Combined with paid work, women's total weekly working time is 57.1 hours, 20.2 percent higher than men's (47.5 hours). This disparity results in an estimated monthly income loss of 223.3 GEL for women due to unpaid work, compared to 50.3 GEL for men.

When scaled to the employed population, these losses amount to 119.8 million GEL per month for women and 34.3 million GEL for men. Despite higher wages for men, women's aggregate losses exceed men's by 249.6 percent (Gelashvili & Okruashvili, 2024).

These findings underscore that the inefficient allocation of human capital leads to significant economic and social costs, diminishing potential welfare gains across the population. While total elimination of these losses may be unfeasible, substantial reductions could improve Georgia's general welfare and economic productivity.

Conclusion

Labour market inequality represents not only a severe social issue but also a significant economic challenge, impacting both individual well-being and the country's economic prosperity. Gender inequality in the labour market can be assessed from various aspects, but the most critical are inequalities in economic inactivity and wage disparities. The high proportion of economically inactive women is mainly due to gender stereotypes, the most prominent being unpaid household and caregiving work. As for gender wage inequality, this can stem from multiple factors, one primary cause being educational attainment. However, in Georgia, women's educational attainment is equal to men's. Experience, which heavily influences pay and employment status, is another critical factor. Based on labour force survey data from the last eight years, calculations show an average work experience of 10.2% for women and 11.4% for men. To account for these causes of gender differences, an adjusted gender pay gap is used. In 2022, the adjusted monthly pay gap was 23.0%, considerably lower than the unadjusted gap of 46.4%. The hourly wage gap, at 15.4%, is also smaller than the monthly gap, as women generally work fewer hours than men, partly due to gender stereotypes. Monthly wage disparities are generally more significant than hourly ones, explained by the higher average hours worked by men. However, in occupations such as specialist-professional roles and machine operators, the hourly wage gap is even more pronounced, reflecting substantial gender inequality and discrimination.

Gender inequality impacts individuals, and the entire economy, as insufficient human capital development is one of the most critical barriers to achieving inclusive economic growth (Bedianashvili, Tsartsidze, Mikeladze, & Gabroshvili, 2023). This issue is even more severe by region, with Tbilisi being the only region achieving desirable employment levels and wages.

Beyond paid activities, gender inequality in unpaid work is significant, particularly in Shida Kartli, Samtskhe-Javakheti, and Kvemo Kartli. Unpaid labour also tends to increase with higher levels of education.

To address and reduce this problem, the first step is to form a legislative framework and enforce it to prevent both direct and indirect gender discrimination in workplaces. Additionally, care services, especially for mothers of young children, should be made universally accessible. Employers should encourage flexible work arrangements for women facing similar challenges, provided organizational functioning is not impacted. Using labour force survey data, a calculation was made regarding the proportion of the workforce working from home in the past four weeks. Before the pandemic, 6.1% of employed women and 3.0% of men worked from home. During the pandemic, these numbers rose to 10.9% for women and 4.6% for men. However, post-pandemic figures declined to 6.7% for women and 3.4% for men, although still higher than pre-pandemic levels, representing a positive step forward. Additionally, creating more job opportunities, particularly for women, is essential.

Considering the above measures would significantly reduce gender imbalance in the labour market, a fundamental component of a prosperous economy and a driver of well-being, especially for women.

Bibliography

Ananiashvili, I. (2012). *Econometrics.* Tbilisi: Meridiani.

Bedianashvili, G., Tsartsidze, M., Mikeladze, N., & Gabroshvili, Z. (2023). Modern Globalization, Human Capital and Economic Growth in Georgia: A Macro Aspect. *Economist.*

Gelashvili, S., & Okruashvili, M. (2024). Statistical analyses of gender disparities in unpaid work in Georgia. *Edelweiss Applied Science and Technology,* 1144-1156.

Geostat. (2020-2021). *Time Use Survey in Georgia.* Retrieved from https://www.geostat.ge/ka/modules/categories/783/drois-gamoqenebis-gamokvleva

Geostat. (2021). *Employment and Unemplyment.* Retrieved from https://www.geostat.ge/ka/modules/categories/683/dasakmeba-umushevroba

Geostat. (2023). *Employment and Unemployment.* Retrieved from https://www.geostat.ge/ka/modules/categories/683/dasakmeba-umushevroba

Guerrero, M. F. (2020-2021). *Time Use Survey in Georgia.* Retrieved from https://www.geostat.ge/ka.

Open Data Watch. (2023). *Gender Data Compass.* Retrieved from https://gdc.opendatawatch.com/

UN Women. (n.d.). *The 17 Goals: Sustainable Development Goals.* Retrieved from United Nations | Peace, dignity and equality on a healthy planet: https://www.un.org/sustainabledevelopment/gender-equality/

Un Women, & Geostat. (2020-2021). *Time Use Survey in Georgia.* Tbilisi.